OBSESSED

A B C D

A Black Girls' Guide to Obsessive Compulsive Disorder

This book is in no way intended to provide a substitution for professional help with OCD or mental illness. This book is my story and some things that helped me however because we are all different, our treatments may very well be different. If you have or if anyone close to you has any of the similarities of mental illness mentioned in this book, please consult my resources section and don't hesitate to seek professional help immediately. You and your families life could depend on it.

Copyright © 2019 by Dionne R. Murphy

Printed in the United States of America

ISBN-13: 9781089380672

OBSESSED

A B C D

A Black Girl's Guide to Obsessive Compulsive Disorder

∞

by Dionne R. Murphy

Foreword

ANXIETY LIVES AMONG US

by Dawniel Winningham

As Dionne's Business Coach and someone who had spent a great deal of time with her, when she first revealed to me that she had struggled with OCD in the past I was very shocked. To know Dionne is to love her. She is bright, bubbly, supportive, friendly and super sweet in a way that you don't see many women nowadays (unless they want something).

So as someone who knows we ALL struggle with something, when Dionne asked me to write the foreword to this book, I wanted to do my research on OCD to put my best foot forward and make her proud. I wanted to honor her as my client and honor her offering to the world.

What I found out blew my mind. I have more in common with Dionne than I would have thought had I not done my research.

You see, my obsession is with food. Because this is Dionne Murphy's book I won't go into it further, but I want you to understand that we ALL experience anxiety in some way or another, it's just that some of us are better handling it than others. And also some of us deal with it in much better ways than others.

But as women, and especially as black women, we have all been taught that it is taboo for us to talk about our misgivings and mental issues, and that we must ALWAYS be secure for everyone else.

Carrying such a cross is enough to drive you crazy by itself. Always needing to be "right" so we don't disappoint others, obsessing over who likes us and who doesn't, and even being willing to risk our health and happiness to make others happy.

I don't know where this comes from in our gender or our race, but what makes it worse is that no one talks about it.

No one studies it. No one is saying 'me too girl', and 'I am struggling with my mind as well'. And so we are forced to sit on the sidelines and think that we are the only ones having anxiety issues when it couldn't be further from the truth.

So whether you have extreme anxiety over relationships, money, or obsessions with food or drugs, or WHATEVER your stress and passion is, I want you from this point on to be honest about it, get some help with it, and when you see someone else struggling with something you don't understand in the mental arena, just reach over, hold their hand, and whisper softly in their ear, "Me too, sister."

Dionne, you are NOT alone. We all struggle, just a different struggle.

I tell people about my weight, and you can SEE my struggle, I just can't see yours.

Love you much,

Coach Dawniel Winningham

' Obsessed with Business and Food

Contents

OBSESSED

A B C D

A Black Girl's Guide to Obsessive Compulsive Disorder

∞

by Dionne R. Murphy

Prologue

AN OBSESSIVE SOCIETY

It is estimated that 2.2 million people, both men and women, suffer from OCD.

My name is Dionne R. Murphy, and I suffer from Obsessive Compulsive Disorder—mostly known by OCD. I used to think I was all alone in my suffering until I started to do research in my quest for answers as I grew older.

Now, to know that 1 in 40 adults and 1 in 100 kids suffer from OCD lets me know that I am not alone. The real problem is that OCD, especially in African American women is often misdiagnosed, if diagnosed at all, and rarely, if ever, spoken about.

Mental illness in the African American community as a whole is something that is rarely spoken of, let alone studied by experts.

I want to share with you some truths about mental illness in the African American Community so that whether you are dealing with OCD, or some other mental illness, you know that you are NOT alone in your journey... and you know it's OK to get help.

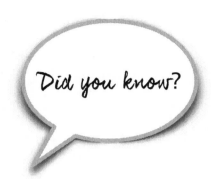

African Americans are 20% more likely to experience mental health problems such as:

☑ Major Depression

☑ Attention Deficit Disorder

☑ Suicide

☑ Post Traumatic Stress Disorder

Factors that increase our mental instability

☑ Homelessness

☑ Being in violent environments

☑ Sexual violence

☑ Death of a loved one

☑ Chronic or serious illness

☑ Divorce

☑ Abandoned by a parent or guardian

☑ Natural disaster

☑ Car accident

☑ Victim of a crime such as robbery

☑ ... any traumatic experience

Factors that keep us from seeking proper care

☑ Mental Health issues are a sign of weakness

☑ Mental Health issues are a punishment from God

☑ Attempts to self-diagnose and self-medicate

☑ Fear of what others think

☑ Relying on Faith, Family, and Friends instead of seeking professional help

☑ Lack of Trust for Health Care Industry

☑ Not able to afford care

☑ Lack of quality healthcare

One of the reasons you don't see OCD on the list is that because there have been VERY few studies conducted on the impacts of OCD in the African American community.

Also because mental illness sometimes manifests as bodily aches and pains, many doctors who are not culturally competent tend to misdiagnose and treat the pain rather than not the source.

I hope this book and the resources included help you to take a different look at mental illness, not only with yourself, but within your family.

You can never be too safe and getting help is critical to living a well-adjusted life, despite your mental setbacks.

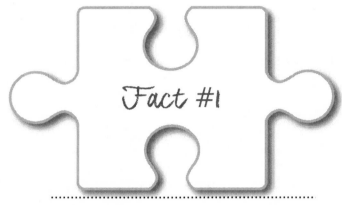

Fact #1

This year alone, there have been over 6.8 million African Americans with a diagnosable mental illness.

Chapter One

AN OBSESSIVE CHILDHOOD

As I was writing my story, I realized that OCD could have been with me as long as I could remember. Most OCD starts in early childhood and develops as you near a young age. In some, it starts earlier than others.

I heard OCD being explained once in comparison to having email. Each of us has intrusive or troublesome thoughts from time to time. Those thoughts are like email. Some of us can "delete" them like junk mail;

while for some of us, the email get STUCK and we read the email or "thought" over and over until we feel the need to "do something" that will delete that email.

Many of you may think it's just someone being germophobic or hoarding, but there are so many more origins for OCD and so many more ways it manifests.

❈ ❈ ❈ ❈

The Belief system that we create as children have been reported to have an impact on OCD.

You will see some of these impacts, in bold, as you read my story. You may even relate to some of them yourself. They are:

1. Inflated responsibility: a belief that one can cause and is responsible for preventing adverse outcomes;

2. Over importance of thoughts (also known as thought-action fusion): the idea that

having a wrong impression can influence the probability of the occurrence of an adverse event or that having a crazy thought (e.g., about doing something) is morally equivalent to actually doing it;

3. Control of ideas: A belief that it is both essential and possible to have total control over one's thoughts;

4. Overestimation of threat: a belief that adverse events are very probable and that they will be particularly bad;

5. Perfectionism: a belief that one cannot make mistakes and that imperfection is unacceptable; and

6. Intolerance for uncertainty: a feeling that it is essential and possible to know, without a doubt, that adverse events won't happen.

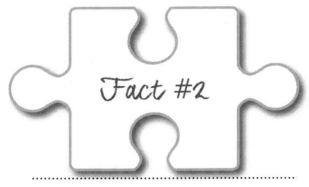

Fact #2

Women are twice as likely to
affected as men for
Generalized Anxiety Disorder
(GAD), Panic Disorder (PD)
and Specific Phobias.

Chapter Two

My Mama's Obsessions

I can remember wanting to be with my mom at all times. I was a Mama's girl. I didn't even want to be at my cousin's house that long because I would think about my mom and wanting to be near her.

I remember as far back as when I was 7 or 8 years old, my cousin - who is 3 years younger than me - would want me to spend the night at her house. My mom was big about not letting us spend the night ANYWHERE,

except my Grandmother's house and two of my aunt's home.

After I agreed to staying the night at my cousin's house, my mom would go on home. Right when my mom would pull out of the driveway, I would feel that frog in my throat, or that pull in my heart that would make me want her to turn around and come back to get me.

Nothing terrible ever happened to me while being at either of my aunt's or grandmother's home, I just wanted to be near my Mama. Nevertheless, my aunt was on the phone within the next hour telling my mom that I wouldn't stay. My Mama could hear me the background crying, so she came and picked me up.

It is possible that because my MOM had a thing about letting me stay with others, I assumed some of that anxiety from her.

Fact #3

The average age of onset of OCD is 19, with 25% of cases occurring by age 14. One-third of affected adults first experienced symptoms in childhood.

Chapter Three

OBSESSED WITH PERFECTION

The earliest memory that I have of my mom is when I used to sleep on her chest. I'm not sure how old I was, but I had to be relatively young. I also have a memory of riding in a long brown Cadillac with my mom and siblings. I had to be around 5 or 6 years old.

I can remember us pulling that Cadillac into the driveway and me being so sleepy that I could barely keep my eyes open. My Mama would carry me up ten wooden steps that led to our Victorian-style home in Mississippi.

Sometimes I would fall asleep as she laid me down and sometimes, I would get up right after she laid me down. My Mama was very protective of myself and two siblings, and she was our nurturer and our protector. My mom did not play any games!

❀ ❀ ❀ ❀

My Mama's word was the final say so. As I entered into my teenage years, my Mama had established that we were not to ask "Why."

If we wanted to go somewhere with our friends and she said 'no', then we knew not to ask why. If we did ask that one-word question, she would say, "Because I said so."

She was firm, and we knew it. I was always the jolly but timid kid. I was still scared of someone telling me 'NO'. Sometimes I would not ask questions just to avoid being told 'NO'.

❋ ❋ ❋ ❋

Perfection. Because of not wanting to be informed NO, I didn't want to do anything wrong.

❋ ❋ ❋ ❋

I barely got spankings from my Mama because it would break my heart to make her mad. So when I did get a spanking, I would be so hurt emotionally afterwards. I just wanted to be under my mom and know that she wasn't mad at me anymore.

❋ ❋ ❋ ❋

Here again, perfection.

❋ ❋ ❋ ❋

Remember when I said my Mama was our nurturer and protector? Well, she protected me to the extent of me not being able to ride my bike outside. She was afraid that I would hurt myself, or that some crazy person would kidnap me.

I can remember being on the large front porch of our Victorian-style home, swinging on this huge wooding swing. I would then go down the steps and begin jumping off the porch, starting with the first one at the bottom.

I used to keep going higher and higher until I reached a level that I could not jump off. I would keep an eye out for any of those white vans that had no side windows, only the driver side window, and the front passenger window.

I would consider those the kidnappers' van and made sure I ran up the stairs and to the front door just in case someone decided to stop and get out of the van to come and get me.

Fear. It had a hold on me, and I didn't even know it.

❋ ❋ ❋ ❋

Here you see the overestimation of threat. Some of it assumed from my mother and from her anxiety at being an over-protector.

❋ ❋ ❋ ❋

I learned to be independent of my Mama. And I learned always to save things for a rainy day because you never know when you might need "that" something.

Everyone knew that I was a Mama's girl and I didn't care. I loved to be around my Mama. I didn't know what I was going to do when I left for college in Louisiana because my Mom would be in Mississippi. But, I made it through. I still consider my Mama my first love to this day.

❀ ❀ ❀ ❀

My Daddy cooked the best steaks. I used to love it when he would come home and cook. He also cooked the best fried green tomatoes.

My Daddy used to have a Jheri curl that had been cut into a mullet style. I can remember the smell of it mixed with Budweiser beer and Kool Filter King cigarettes. These were his staples.

I can remember him having this scar in the palm of one of his hands. He used to tell me the story about him getting wounded in Vietnam. I used to love listening to his stories. I would hang on to his every word.

My daddy worked for a company that installed jukeboxes, pool tables, and video games into people's homes and businesses. He would bring me pool balls, cues, and pool sticks home. We also had a jukebox in our home that we played regularly as well as a huge Arcade game of Pac Man and a shooting game. We rarely played those arcade games in the house because they would trip the circuit breaker.

❀ ❀ ❀ ❀

I loved watching wrestling with my Daddy and my brother. We used to get up on some Saturday mornings to watch it. I cherished those times that my Daddy would be home to watch wrestling with us.

I couldn't wait until my dad would get back home. Sometimes it would be two to three days before I would see him. Not because he was working late, but because he was out doing his thing.

❀ ❀ ❀ ❀

I asked him for a bike one time, and I knew he was going to get it for me. Every time he came home, I would hear his orange and white pickup truck pull up outside. I listened intently for the truck door to shut, and I would wait to hear his footsteps coming up those ten wooden steps.

I would imagine that I heard the chain rattle on the bike as he would walk up the stairs. And when he got to the porch, I would be standing in the hallway waiting for him to come through the front door.

The door would open, and I would see him stumbling in. There was no bike in sight. All the extra noise I heard while he would climb the front porch stairs would be him stumbling and dropping change on the steps. It would fall out of his pockets.

I waited and waited for months for him to walk through the door with a bike, and it never happened. He and my mom separated when I was 9 years old, and that was the end of me smelling the Jheri curl mixed with beer and Kool Filter King cigarettes.

My dad had a girlfriend, and she had nieces and nephews. I would always wonder where my daddy would be; but on the inside, I knew exactly where he was because of the arguments I would hear between my Mama and Daddy as I hid around the corner out of sight.

Neither of them knew I was listening. I learned a lot about both my Mama and Daddy from those arguments. My dad would do things for his girlfriend's nieces and nephews that he wouldn't do for us. I remember him explaining to my Mama why he would buy them fireworks and didn't buy us any. He said that he knew my Mama would get them for us anyway.

❀ ❀ ❀ ❀

My Mama never talked wrong about my Daddy to us. She always told us, "Good daddy or bad daddy, but that is still your daddy."

She said to us that if we saw our daddy on the street or if he needed some money or if he was hungry, help him out because he was still our daddy.

I used to watch how my cousins would interact with their dads and wish I had that. A few of those times I would go into the bathroom and cry because I wanted to be playing with or just talking to my daddy. But I couldn't because he was with his girlfriend and her family.

Perfection again, I wanted my life to be just like others and because it wasn't, I felt to blame.

As I grew older, I used to go and visit my Daddy here and there—when his girlfriend was not around. I couldn't wait for him to hug me and kiss on the forehead. It didn't matter to me that he wasn't living with us or that he was living with another woman who wasn't his wife/my Mama—I just wanted him to hug me and give me a kiss on the forehead.

That did not happen often, but when it did, I cherished it. I never really saw my dad after I left home for college. I would talk to him here and there on the phone, and it would be only for a few minutes. He never really wanted to speak for long.

❀ ❀ ❀ ❀

When I became an adult, it was the same kind of relationship with my Daddy - distant and sporadic. I can remember on Father's day in June of 2006, I spoke with him on the phone, and he apologized for his actions throughout the years.

We had also discussed me going to visit him for his birthday. I was so excited! He had moved to Minnesota to live with his brother a few years prior. I called him to get details so that I could plan my trip, but I got no answer. I kept trying, and he didn't answer. I even called him on his birthday, and he didn't answer.

I let the disappointment go but secretly wondered what was going on. In December of 2006, six months later, my dad passed away, and I was crushed!

I recalled trying to get in contact with him, but he avoided my calls. I never got a chance to have a conversation with him as a grown up. I knew that he loved my siblings and me, but what made him not want to be around us?

For the longest time, I always had thoughts of what it would have been like to see him for one last time. I can't even tell you the last time that I saw my Daddy in person.

I've always wanted to have my Dad in my life, no matter the circumstances between him and my mother, but that didn't happen. It just never happened.

So for years, I carried the burden of something being wrong with ME as why my Daddy stopped coming around. And I never got a chance to ask him that burning question as an adult from when I was just a little girl.

Perfection again! I am sure this was a stressor for my OCD. Not being able to have closure with my father before he passed away. I am always wanting my mom and dad back together.

Fact #4

It is possible that African Americans with the most severe OCD, especially those with unusual obsessions or compulsions, may be misdiagnosed as psychotic.

Chapter Four

OBSESSED WITH SUPERSTITIONS

I loved my grandmother, and she was our second mom; she is my Mama's mom. I never got a chance to meet my Dad's mom.

I can remember being a little girl laying on a pillow across my grandmother's lap as she put me to sleep. I am not sure of my age, but I was young enough to be able to fit onto a pillow in her lap.

We would spend a lot of time at my grandmother's house because my mom worked long hours to be able to take care of us. The times that we would spend the night at my grandmother's house, I remember waking up and watching my aunt comb her hair.

My aunt would get her hair pressed (or straightened) and use those sponge rollers to curl her hair. I would watch my aunt take those rollers out and comb her hair to the back, and then push it to the front to mold it into her hairstyle for the day.

She was a teacher that worked out of town (about 30 minutes away), and she used to get up early in the morning to get dressed. I would watch her until she left to go to work.

I could not wait until I was old enough to be able to roll my hair on the black sponge rollers so that I could take them out and comb my curls to the back only to push them up to the front.

The smell of floral perfume trickled past my nose, and that let me know that my aunt had completed her routine of getting ready for work.

❀ ❀ ❀ ❀

I remember this one particular time that after my aunt finished getting ready, she made her way to the kitchen to chat with my grandmother before she left for work. I remember her sitting her big black oversized purse on the floor, and my grandmother immediately telling her, "Girl pick your purse up off of the floor or you are going to be broke!"

It's one of those superstitions that stuck with me, and I believed it for years into my adulthood. My family was big on superstitious beliefs. Some of the things I grew up hearing were fearful to me.

So needless to say, I would follow the rules of what was being taught. It was only then when I became an adult that I learned to do away with the superstitious thinking and beliefs because it caused me high anxiety.

❀ ❀ ❀ ❀

My cousins and I loved going outside at my grandmother's house. We would play in the yard until she made us come inside. I also remember us waiting for the mailman to come.

Back in the day, the mailman would come up to the porch and put the mail in the mailbox right next to the front door. My two cousins and I would be there waiting for him because he had tons of beige, blue, and red rubber bands of all thicknesses at the base of the gear shift on the steering wheel of his mail truck.

We used to ask him for rubber bands each time, and he would give each of us a few. No particular reason, we just wanted the rubber bands to play with.

As I grew older, my cousin and I would sometimes stay the night at the aunt's house who I used to watch do her hair. She would make us broccoli and cheese as well as cheese spaghetti. We loved to have sleepovers at this aunt's house because we could have the freedom to watch TV all night and play dress up in her clothes, jewelry, and shoes.

❀ ❀ ❀ ❀

I had some wonderful aunts and uncles. They indeed showed love to all of the kids. I had two uncles that were more like fathers to me, but neither of them filled that longing that I had for my real father.

Both of my uncles were there to take me places and have conversations with me that I cherished. But deep down, I still had a longing and need for my Dad, who wasn't anywhere around - he had moved on to his new family.

One of those uncles had children of his own and still took the time to fix on my car, gave me another car to have during the last of my college years, helped me move out of my apartment and into my house as an adult, and he Christened my baby.

The other Uncle did not have children. He was the one to work all of the time, but would still come and spend time with us on the weekend. He would bring us 50 pounds or more of crawfish every time he came to visit during the spring and summer.

He also made sure I went to London, England during my senior year in high school. He made sure I went to college with no financial worries. With all of that, neither of them was able to fill that longing that I had for my real father.

I used to look at my cousins playing with their dads as a child. It would make me cry at times, but no one knew. I would go to the restroom to wipe away my tears and get myself together. I always used to wonder what was wrong with me. Why didn't my dad want to do me the same way? My uncles and aunts were there for me, my siblings, and my Mama, but there was still this gaping hole in my heart for my Dad.

Fact #5

African Americans
experience OCD at
equivalent rates as the
general population, but are
underrepresented in OCD
treatment clinics and
research studies.

Chapter Five

OBSESSED WITH TAPPING

I loved going to school at Louisiana Tech University. Education was my chance to gain my independence, meet tons of new people, prepare for my future, and have fun.

I had always earned fantastic grades. I was active in dance, band, and track and field all through junior high and high school.

Around the age of 13, it was brought to my attention that I would walk differently or tap on things. Once that was brought to my attention, I began to try and hide those actions. My family was the ones that noticed and brought it to my attention. And I would say that I didn't know why I did that.

I tried to play it down so they would think I was a kid just doing some crazy things. Even as I grew older, my cousins would make comments about me doing that "tapping stuff." I thought I was hiding it, but someone was still noticing it.

Once I became an adult, I asked my Mama and my sister if they used to see me doing those actions as a child, and they both confirmed it—I never knew they noticed. They never really said anything, it was the other family members what were the most vocal about it.

❋ ❋ ❋ ❋

When I made it to college, I was aware that I genuinely had to try and hide the "tapping stuff" because I knew people would eventually think I was crazy. But that only made it escalate.

If I didn't touch something the right amount of times or walk a certain number of steps or made sure the left side of my body felt equal to the right side of my body, I would be afraid that I was going to get some bad news.

So, I would do whatever it took to fight off that anxiety. I can call it anxiety because I now know, as an adult, what it was. But growing up, I didn't know what it was back then. I would be almost late to class trying to fight off the anxiety.

I would often wonder, what is wrong with me?! I was a massive believer in superstition, so I made sure not to split poles, step on cracks; I didn't put my purse on the floor; I made sure nobody swept my feet; I definitely didn't want the black cat to cross my path, and this was only a few of the superstitious ideas that were embedded in my head.

The anxiety was getting to me because it pooled over into my school work. I was so afraid of being kicked out of school for poor grades that I immersed myself in my studies.

I did venture to have fun here and there, but I was right back into the books. I made sure to hide that "tapping stuff" because I was very aware that people would notice—even if I thought they didn't.

SO I would make sure only to do it when I was alone in my dorm room or do everything in my head when I would be walking to class, to lunch, to band practice, etc.

I would be making the patterns in my head. I would keep walking until I got it right and would try to play it off like I was in another world just in case I walked past the building I was supposed to be going in.

Thinking about it today, I used to always wonder what is wrong with me?

I graduated in 2002, and my family was there to celebrate with me. You guessed it by now, my dad wasn't at my graduation, making the wound of something being wrong with me even deeper and hurt more.

Fact #6

One in 5 people is affected
by mental illness.

Chapter Six

Obsessed with Tragedy

I moved to Houston, Texas in October 2002. I had only one relative there, and I lived with him and his wife for three months.

I then moved into my apartment. It was so liberating finally to be able to do the "tapping stuff" as much as I needed to because I was in a place where I knew no one.

Even if I slipped up and did a tapping ritual where someone could see, they probably wouldn't pay too much attention to it because I didn't know them. This was all in my head, though [thinking no one would notice].

Tapping and repeating specific touching patterns began to consume me. It got so bad that I would be late for work just because I could not get the keys out of my apartment door. I had to get the pattern and numbers just right before I could take the key out of the lock.

I would get so frustrated and cry because I couldn't just walk away. The obsession was just too strong. What is wrong with me?!!

This pattern went on for years. Ten more years to be exact!

❀ ❀ ❀ ❀

In 2003, I enrolled in graduate school. I met even more people. I was working full-time and going to school. This time, school was a breeze for me. I had already graduated once, so I knew I could do it again. Especially since I graduated with a Biomedical Engineering degree, this Masters of Business Administration (MBA) should be a breeze. And it was.

❋ ❋ ❋ ❋

In 2006, I had some extraordinary things to happen in my life as well as a tragedy. You see, I was always trying to prevent bad things from happening when I would do my tapping and touching. For the most part it worked—at least it worked in my head. I thought I was really able to keep as much bad news at bay by following my routine. I couldn't stop it. I was obsessed with it. Literally.

Well, in 2006, I bought my first home, and I graduated with my MBA. My family was there to support both of those accomplishments. But later in 2006, as mentioned before, my dad passed away.

I didn't prevent that from happening. I would always wonder why he never picked up my phone call. I cried because I said I tried to call and visit, but he never answered. I was able to file that away in the back of my mind and move forward, but deep down, I blamed me for every bad thing that ever happened.

Perhaps I didn't tap enough. Maybe I missed a tap, maybe I was crying too hard and missed a routine or overlooked it somehow. Whatever I did, I knew that it was all me. It was my fault. Yet still, I couldn't figure out what was wrong with me.

Fact #7

Only about one-quarter of
African Americans seek
mental health care,
compared to 40% of whites.

Chapter Seven

OBSESSED WITH OBSESSIONS

Time went on, and I continued to tap and touch. I realized that something was indeed wrong with what I was doing.

OCD holds your mind hostage. Help is not on the way. There isn't a button to push to alert someone and let them know that you are being held hostage. So what do you do?

Well, I just kept doing what I knew to do best, and that was to continue to tap and touch until the fear temporarily went away.

At that time, I never knew that tapping and touching was a form of OCD. Many people attribute OCD to excessive hand washing or people who need to have everything sparkling clean or in a straight line.

That was not me at all so you can imagine why it took me so long to figure out that this condition of tapping and touching was OCD.

The form of OCD I have is the COMPULSION to touch or move things. My compulsions are ritualistic and superstitious. I would do the following:

☑ Touch things a certain number of times

☑ Touch things until if felt symmetrical

☑ Repeat activities such as standing up, sitting down, walking through doorways, stepping in a particular manner for a certain number of times until I felt right

☑ Looking at things in a certain way

☑ Go through step patterns in my head while walking

☑ Touch things in a specific design

☑ Make really quiet sounds in a design with my voice

☑ Twisting doorknobs a certain amount of times before opening or closing the door

These are just a few. I felt the need to have to do those rituals to keep from having something "bad" happen to me, my family, etc. These are intrusive thoughts. Intrusive thoughts are obsessions. Y'all, this was pure HELL and I could not stop it.

❋ ❋ ❋ ❋

I can remember trying my best to lock my apartment door another day until I was actually late for work. I was stuck. I could not get the pattern right so I could not leave the door alone. I had to turn the key a certain number of times until it FELT RIGHT. IF I didn't do this, I would think someone was going to call me with horrible news about one of my family members.

So to keep this from happening I had to turn the key an excessive number of times. This was just one of many episodes.

Can you imagine living like this every day?

Fact #8

Studies have found that it takes an average of 17 years from the time OCD begins for people to obtain appropriate treatment.

Chapter Eight
FREEDOM FROM OBSESSIONS

I learned to build up a tolerance to my anxiety. To my fear! I had to tell myself over and over and over again that nothing was going to happen to my family if I didn't do the compulsion.

I learned to let the anxiety build, and I had to resist during the urge until the tension began to decrease or cease. Once I successfully did this ONE time, I experienced a feeling like none other.

I was able to prevail over fear and anxiety for once. I then started to do that more often until it almost became second nature to me.

You see, I say ALMOST. I still have the urges, but I know how to overcome them. I overcome the urges EVERY SINGLE DAY. But, my life is more joyful now. This is why I am so bubbly, positive, joyful and happy.

I lived my life in a mental prison from age 13 until I was 33-years-old. I was granted parole in 2012 and have been out on excellent behavior ever since!

IT IS POSSIBLE TO BE FREE MENTALLY.

❋ ❋ ❋ ❋

One day in 2012, a coworker of mine introduced me to a man (mentor) that was teaching women a class about knowing who they are. I decided to take this eight-week course, and I am so glad I did! It helped me change my life!

This man taught me that I have control over what I felt, what I believed, what I thought, and more. He told me I had the power on the inside of me to do ANYTHING!

I heard and read this before, but it stayed on the surface. I didn't really "get it" until I sat under his tutelage. That changed when my mentor told me HOW to access and activate the power within me.

I remember thinking that if I truly had control over all of that, then I can surely control my anxiety and the feelings of bad things happening. This is real y'all!

And in typical formation, I went to work! I believed. I spoke my healing. I believed more. I expressed my healing more. Then I visualized what it would feel like to do something as simple as turning off a light switch and walking away without flipping it 32 times.

Anytime I feel an intrusive thought trying to creep in when I touch something, I replace that thought with a positive and healing affirmation. I talk to myself and say, "Nothing is going to happen."

I was able to free myself! It felt so good the first time I was able to bypass tapping and touching and keep on moving. Like I said, when I did this the first time and realized that nothing terrible happened, I cried. I wept.

But there was something in my mind that made me want to test that out time and time again. I had to, I wanted to remain free, and I did.

❊ ❊ ❊ ❊

Relaxation and minimizing stress can help you cope with OCD. For me, keeping negativity at bay is crucial. I don't like to hear people talk about negative situations or their beliefs that do not line up with what I believe. I have to protect my mind, I must control what enters and exits it.

Having certain hobbies help me to cope with OCD. I love making and creating things with my hands, and it gives my mind a break from the day-to-day happenings around me.

Fitness is another great coping mechanism for my OCD. When I work out, anxiety and fear do not even enter my head space. I go into a zone where I want to do my best and get the best results for my health and my body.

Being Mindful is another way to cope with OCD. I pay very close attention to my thoughts, to my body, and to whatever is around me. I take note of how my thoughts make me feel. I take note of how my body responds to certain elements, and I take note of things that surround me and how they make me feel. If something does not feel right to me, I make sure to remove myself from that particular position or environment.

❀ ❀ ❀ ❀

OCD is a mental illness, and we as African Americans do not deal or claim mental illness. It is just something that does not happen to us, right? Wrong!!

I am so thankful that I was able to learn how to deal with my OCD and I want to help others do the same. I continue to practice my mental FREEDOM daily. Since I know how to combat those urges and thoughts, I am living my best life!

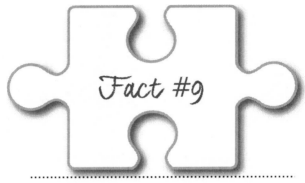

Fact #9

According to the American Psychological Association, African Americans account for 5.3% of the psychology workforce.

Chapter Nine

CAUSE OF OBSESSIVE COMPULSIVE DISORDER

OCD can result from specific triggers be it behavioral, cognitive, neurological, genetic and environmental factors. It usually begins in late childhood or early adolescence.

Research has also shown that OCD is a result of genetic and hereditary factors. Distorted beliefs can cause OCD. You see, I had distorted views from the beginning with all of the superstitious sayings from my family.

I used to think something was wrong with me because my dad left us. Why didn't he want to be with us? Why didn't he ever keep his promise and buy me that bike? Why couldn't he play with me as my cousins' dad would play with them?

That made me think something was wrong with me and it was a lot for a young impressionable little girl to put on herself, with no one to tell her differently.

❀ ❀ ❀ ❀

Forms of OCD

There are many different types of OCD which include:

☑ Checking

☑ Contamination/Mental Contamination

☑ Hoarding

☑ Intrusive Thoughts

☑ Symmetry/Ordering

I know that the form of OCD that resonates with me is the intrusive thoughts. As I look back, I see hoarding is within my family amongst several family members. I even see a little bit of that in myself.

NO matter the form of OCD that someone has, it can be managed. It takes support from those closest to you, and it takes someone to be in your corner who is not going to judge you.

It also takes someone who has the knowledge to help you overcome your FEARS. For me, that person was my mentor. I cannot stress enough how life changing being able to overcome a compulsion for the first time.

I was actively engaging in my compulsions
for 20 years!   I am now 40 years old, and I
have been able to manage my OCD and be
free for the past seven years!!!

❋ ❋ ❋ ❋

One of my missions is to be able to help
people set their minds free just as my mentor
did for me. Mental health is a part of your
complete health and wellness. The health
and wellness coach inside of me wants
people to be healthy in their minds and
body. This is the total package!

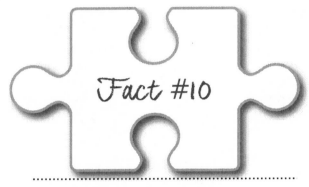

Fact #10

Black/African Americans hold beliefs related to stigma, psychological openness, and help-seeking, which in turn affects their coping behaviors.

Chapter Ten

OBSESSED WITH MYSELF

To be healthy in your mind and body, you have to take care of yourself first so that you can show up in YOUR life.

To care for your family, YOU have to be well. To show up at your job and do your best, you have to be well. To show up and run your business, you have to be well. Being selfish is okay!

Here is my formula to help you be
S E L F I S H .

☑ Stop putting yourself off. Do something
for yourself for a change.

☑ Expect to work at your goals. Whatever
you want to accomplish, know that you
are going to have to put in work.

☑ Lifestyle - make this a lifestyle change.
Make it a habit to make yourself a
priority within your life.

☑ Free - wrap your mind around the fact
that you are free to create the life you
want to have. You have the ability and
power to do so.

☑ Ignore the urge to let what others think
of you matter as you are putting yourself
first.

☑ Stay the course. Quit quitting and giving
up. You are well deserving of your best
life. You are well worthy to be set free.

You are well worthy of being first for a change.

☑ Hold yourself accountable, keep your word. Honor your word. Know that you can do just what you have set out to do and accomplish.

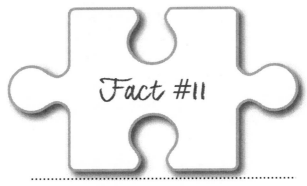

Fact #11

While the implementation of the Affordable Care Act has helped to close the gap in uninsured individuals, 15.9% of Black/African Americans, versus 11.1% of whites, Americans were still uninsured in 2014.

Chapter Eleven

BEYOND OBSESSION

The way you look at EVERYTHING is IMPORTANT. Stop focusing on what you don't want and ask for what you DO want... Ask and it is given, so be careful and mean it. Be mindful of those limiting beliefs because they can take root and develop into something more, hence OCD.

OCD might not be the LIMITING BELIEF on a page in your book of life, but you have a limiting belief of some sort.

Maybe it believes that you can't start your practice because you didn't go to business school. Perhaps it's not able to apply for that out-of-state scholarship because you don't believe you are a good writer. You didn't pass English Comp 101 with an A or B, so now you think you don't have the "right" words to say. LIMITED BELIEF.

❋ ❋ ❋ ❋

Maybe you don't want to major in what you want to major in only because no one in your family ever thought about being that engineer, Marketing Manager, or speech pathologist. You thought, oh I'll major in general studies so that I can get a little bit of everything. LIMITED BELIEF.

❋ ❋ ❋ ❋

Maybe you are thinking you should drop out because juggling being a single parent in college and working a job all while trying to meet your assignment deadlines is too hard.

You may think to yourself, "My Aunt Rachel did okay and she dropped out, so I guess I can drop out and make it just like her." LIMITED BELIEF.

❊ ❊ ❊ ❊

You see, we place limits on ourselves all of the time. Most of the time we are not aware that we are limiting ourselves. Your mindset is everything. How you react to situations is everything.

Become more aware of your self-talk. Watch your words. When you catch yourself entertaining a limiting belief, fear, or superstition, find it at that moment and replace it with something opposite of what is limiting your view.

YOUR words are powerful when they align with your thoughts and emotions. You are responsible for your happiness.

Sometimes you have to take time to experience the quietness. Get into a place where you will not be bothered (your closet, your bathroom, your garage, etc.). Begin to focus on what it is that you want out of life. Picture yourself being in that position or place. Keep that vision at the forefront of your mind and claim it.

Please take the time and focus on yourself now and then. You want to feel good. There's nothing like feeling GOOD.

❀ ❀ ❀ ❀

Have you ever just had a moment where you were so happy and you didn't know why? Things could be chaotic all around you, but you still felt good. That is the good feeling that I am talking about. There is nothing like it.

❀ ❀ ❀ ❀

Create your next hour, create your tomorrow. Create your future. You have the power to do so. God gave it to each one of us.

There aren't any limits to what you can be, do or have. I'll say this again: Free your mind! Replace those negative thoughts with positive ones. Watch your words. Be mindful of what you are saying to yourself about yourself.

You know, someone once told me that it takes 21 days to develop a habit. Repeating something for 21 days will be a part of your everyday routine if you continue to do it.

One thing I want you to get used to doing is talking to yourself in the mirror. Reaffirm positive beliefs while looking at yourself in the mirror. Believe it. Then go out and live your life being FREE.

Start now and CREATE YOUR NEW LIFE.

❀ ❀ ❀ ❀

#OCD is NOT FUNNY

One of the reasons that people struggle to get help with OCD and many of the other mental illnesses is the worry over the social stigma attached to mental illness.

The truth of the matter is that 1 in 5 individuals may be OK on the outside and struggling with mental illness on the inside.

The inability to be able to discuss it socially and to get support openly only worsens the situation.

That's why hashtags like #OCD on social media as it relates to being super neat are not funny. It's not unusual to call people crazy or retarded or many other "terms of endearment" that we have picked up as a society to use in "fun."

If we were to take a closer look at ourselves and the fact that none of us are perfect, I am sure we would be more understanding and supportive of others.

Here are some things that make mental wellness taboo

- ☑ Afraid of being ostracized or left out of activities

- ☑ Fearful of being judged by others

- ☑ Afraid of being talked about

- ☑ Afraid of being watched once the mental illness is known

- ☑ Afraid of mental health professionals

- ☑ Afraid to use pharmaceutical medications

- ☑ Fearful of having conversations with strangers in support groups

All of these things make us more likely to self-medicate, which drives up the incidents of drug and alcohol abuse in our community.

A lot of what we see as drug abuse in the black community is more so mental illness as a way of "fixing" their problems.

But because of the stigma attached to African Americans and drugs, most people don't know the difference. My mission is to change this narrative and educate our communities about mental health.

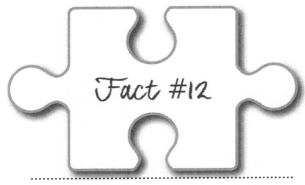

Fact #12

In 2011, 54.3% of adult
Black/African Americans
with a major depressive
episode received treatment,
compared with 73.1% of
adult white Americans.

Chapter Twelve
OBSESSED WITH EVERYONE

Surprisingly the very ones that are supposed to be so strong are the ones MOST impacted by mental health issues: women.

It is a well-known stereotype that women have to be "strong" and "push through." That very stereotype causes us to harbor mental issues to ourselves and contributes to more heart disease and other health impacts for African American Women.

Because women, and African American women in particular, are so busy taking care of everyone else—their kids, the men in their life, the people on their job, their parents, and too many more to name such as the people at church and in the community—it is no wonder that their self-care, both emotionally and physically, often falls to the bottom of the priority list.

As women, we must remember that our inability to take care of ourselves limits our ability to take care of our families in the long run.

There is nothing S E L F I S H about taking care of ourselves. It includes such essential self-care habits as:

☑ Getting a full night's sleep, aim for at least 7 hours. When you have a lack of rest, your mood is not stable and you are less productive.

☑ Get more exercise. Although it may seem complicated, aim for at least 30 minutes of exercise each day. This will boost your feel-good levels and is enough to help some ward off depression.

☑ Focus on better eating habits. Reduce fried foods and sweets, and work on eating more fresh fruits, vegetables, and lean meat.

☑ Be social. Focus on spending time and talking to other individuals that may be going through the same things that you are. It helps you understand you are not alone and keeps you from bottling in all of your emotions.

☑ Say NO. It helps to make a list of things that are most important to you so that other people's to-do list doesn't become a priority for you so much so that you can't take care of you.

☑ Be still. Sometimes it is good to spend time doing nothing. Try yoga. Meditate. Take long walks and even longer baths. Schedule your YOU time and don't allow anyone or anything to take it away.

❋ ❋ ❋ ❋

None of these things replaces help from a professional. If you notice any changes in the following areas, or even if something doesn't FEEL right with you, know that you OWE it to yourself to seek qualified help:

☑ Sleeping more than usual, or wanting to do nothing but sleep

☑ Eating more or less than usual

☑ Feelings of hopelessness or emptiness

☑ Not able to enjoy your usually favorite things

- ☑ Unexplained mood swings

- ☑ Lack of focus

- ☑ Impressions of your life being out of control

Keep in mind that these feelings don't mean something is WRONG with you. Sometimes life is just too much for us to handle alone.

Remember that the things you do for yourself NOW are the things that will help your family survive WITH you later.

And your family is MUCH better off with you!

Fact #13

Adult Black/African Americans are more likely to have feelings of sadness, hopelessness, and worthlessness than are adult whites.

Chapter Thirteen
Obsessed with Fame

After the suicide of megastar actor and comedian, Robin Williams, who suffered for a long time with a mental illness, many celebrities have opened up about mental illness. I hope this helps the world to see that we are all people and that all people have problems.

Janet Jackson opened up about struggling with anxiety and depression in her 30's. She attributed her feelings to:

- ☑ Low self-esteem coming from not feeling good enough as a child

- ☑ Personal opinions of failing to meet impossibly high standards

- ☑ The stress of racism and sexism

Mariah Carey opened up about her struggle with being bipolar and how she felt she had to hide it for so long

Gabourey Sidibe battled depression and panic attacks for years when she finally decided to get help. She realized that this was not something she had to do alone.

Chrissy Teigen, wife of John Legend, discussed post-partum, anxiety, and even physical pain concerning her mental impacts.

Many of these celebrities have a lot in common with us, and I hope that by sharing this list you understand that if they can get help, you can, too, and you should.

> See the complete list of celebrities of all colors, genders, and ages here: https://people.com/health/stars-who-have-mental-illnesses-mental-health-issues/

- THE END -

About the Author

Dionne R. Murphy is a former Educator, Biomedical Engineer, Fitness Competitor, Business Owner and Author. With over 20 years of experience in the health and wellness arena, she is not a stranger to hard work and dedication in order to reach one's fullest potential.

Dionne was born in Vicksburg, Mississippi and earned a Bachelor of Science in Biomedical Engineering and an MBA from Louisiana Tech University and Texas

Southern University, respectively. In addition to sharing her talents and knowledge within the wellness circuit, Dionne is also a Global Strategic Sourcing professional within a Fortune 500 organization.

As the owner of Her Virtual Gym, Dionne helps busy women fit quick workouts and healthy habits into their busy daily schedules all from the comfort of their homes. She educates on self-care, as well as promotes why health and wellness must become a priority in one's life. Her goal is to remove all excuses from women who seek to improve their health and wellness, and turn it into a lifestyle.

Visit her website at: hervirtualgym.com

Download your free gift at bit.ly/putmefirst

Resources

1. National Alliance on Mental Illness:
   https://www.nami.org/find-support/
   diverse-communities/african-americans

2. Questions for African Americans to ask
   your Mental Health Provider

   ▸ Have you treated other African
     Americans?

   ▸ Have you received training in cultural
     competence or on African American
     mental health?

   ▸ How do you see our cultural backgrounds
     influencing our communication and my
     treatment?

   ▸ How do you plan to integrate my beliefs
     and practices in my treatment?

3. How to get help on a budget. If finances
   are preventing you from finding help,
   contact a local health or mental health
   clinic or your local government to see
   what services you qualify. You can find

contact information online at findtreatment.samhsa.gov or by calling the National Treatment Referral Helpline at 800-662-HELP (4357).

4. Do I have OCD? Here is a great test to screen yourself for OCD. However, if you think you have any mental issues, please seek professional help immediately: https://www.additude.com/screener-obsessive-compulsive-disorder-symptoms-test-adults/

5. Books and Videos on OCD and Mental Illness

   ▸ "Shook" by Charlamagne the God

6. Book List from the International OCD Foundation: https://iocdf.org/books/ #Aspergers

7. Annual OCD Conference: https://www.ocd2019.org/

8. Anxiety and Depression Association of America: https://adaa.org/about-adaa/press-room/facts-statistics

9. International OCD Foundation: https://iocdf.org/expert-opinions/african-americans-with-ocd-a-hidden-population-and-new-research/

10. National Center for Biotechnology Information: https://www.ncbi.nlm.nih.gov/pmc/articles/PMC3253913/

11. Zencare: https://www.zencare.co/provider-identity/black/therapists

12. Mental Health America: http://www.mentalhealthamerica.net/african-american-mental-health